TREBLE CLEF

for the cello

by Cassia Harvey

CHP442

©2024 C. Harvey Publications®
All Rights Reserved.
www.charveypublications.com - print books & free sheet music blog
www.learnstrings.com - downloadable books & chamber music

Table of Contents

Section	Page
How to Learn Treble Clef with This Book	3
How the Book Works	4
Note Charts	5
Bass Clef to Treble Clef	6
Positions Across Strings	22
Tenor Clef to Treble Clef	26
Treble Clef and Thumb Position	30
Scales and Arpeggios	34
Octave Shifts	39
Harmonics as Landmarks	40
"False" Treble Clef: Reading an Octave Lower	42
Learning a Beethoven Quartet Excerpt	47
Learning Dvorak "American Quartet" Excerpts	48

How to Learn Treble Clef with This Book

Play with Awareness

This book will work the best when you play with awareness. Be mindful of the name of each note, what it looks like on the staff, and where it is played on the cello. Be especially careful when you see a clef change; many of these were written to be tricky and to force the player to stay aware.

Remember

Try to remember what the notes look like on the staff as you play. Use letter names (C, D) when possible. Knowing the letter names of notes will help you apply key signatures to music properly.

Pick Landmark Notes

Pick your landmark notes: notes that you easily recognize in treble clef and on the cello. Here are some favorite landmark notes:

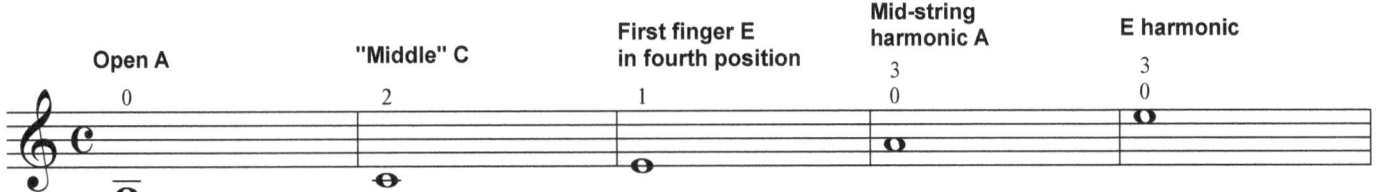

When is Treble Clef Used?

Treble clef is often seen in advanced cello music that goes above fourth position and is used to make the high notes appear lower and more readable.

Who Needs to Know Treble Clef?

Intermediate students should start to learn treble clef around the time they start learning three-octave scales and slightly before they start thumb position. Composers and publishers of advanced solo, chamber, and orchestral music assume that cellists can read all three clefs (bass, tenor, and treble) fluently.

©2024 C. Harvey Publications® All Rights Reserved.

How the Book Works

Reading and Using Multiple Staves

In this book, some of the notes are first written on a double or keyboard staff. This helps you see how bass clef connects to treble clef. The notes are then written again on a single staff so that you can practice reading them as they would usually occur in cello music.

When you see the notes on the double staff, play each note in order, switching between staves when necessary. To begin with, arrows are included to help your eye adjust.

Why All the Clef Changes?

This treble clef method is like boot camp for your brain. The many clef changes force your brain to instantly recognize the notes that the book is trying to teach.

While it's not always a comfortable way to learn, the multiple clef change method is effective at commanding attention, especially in light of the scattered way our brains process information in this electronic age.

What Do the Roman Numerals Refer To?

Roman Numerals refer to strings, not positions.
I = A string   II = D string   III = G string   IV = C string

Why Aren't There More Finger Numbers?

Finger numbers can keep you from recognizing and remembering the notes. When there are no finger numbers, use fingering that makes the most sense to you. If a roman numeral is under a note, play the note on that string.

Reading Treble Clef an Octave Lower

At the end of the book, there is a section on reading treble clef an octave (eight notes) lower. This skill is required for some solo and chamber music that is still published with "false" treble clef that is supposed to be read an octave lower.

©2024 C. Harvey Publications® All Rights Reserved.

Treble Clef for the Cello

Note Charts

These first two charts show you how bass clef connects to treble clef. In the chart on the right, it shows how treble clef can be seen as a continuation of bass clef.

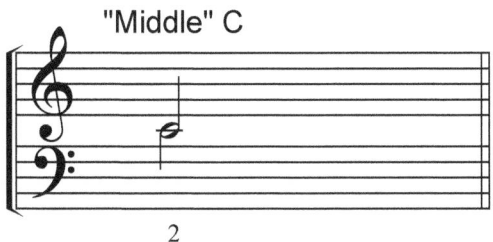

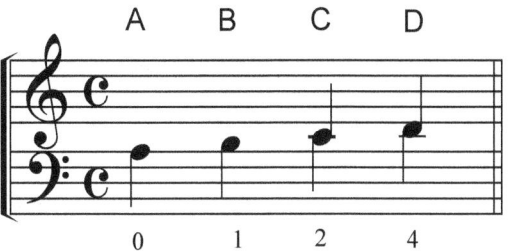

Bass and Treble Clef Chart

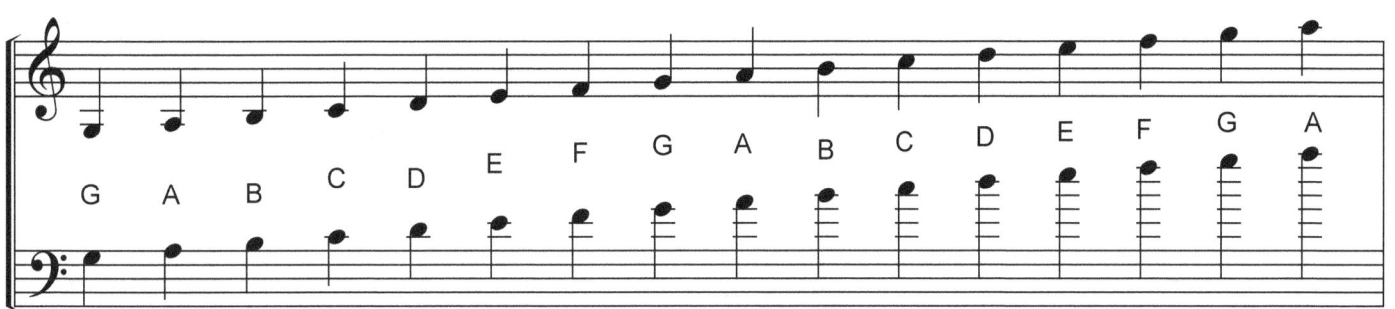

Tenor and Treble Clef Chart

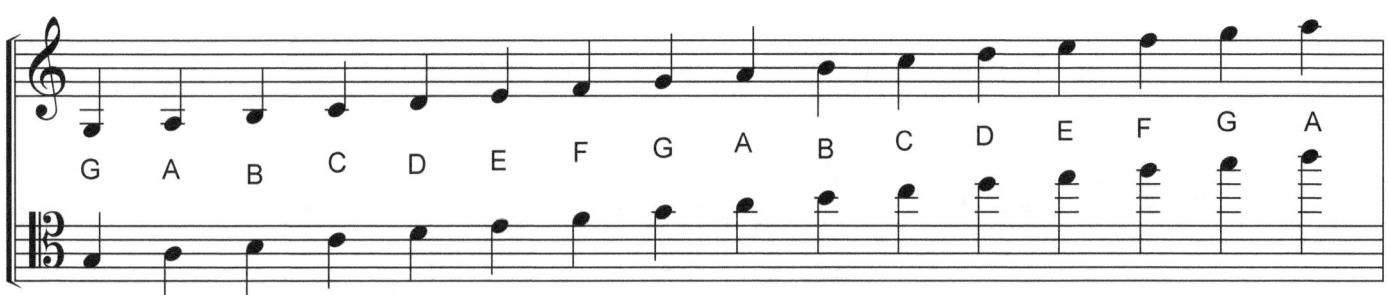

1a. Treble Clef Connections Starting on G (score form)

Each measure on this line has the same notes. Play and read with
awareness, seeing how each note looks in treble clef.

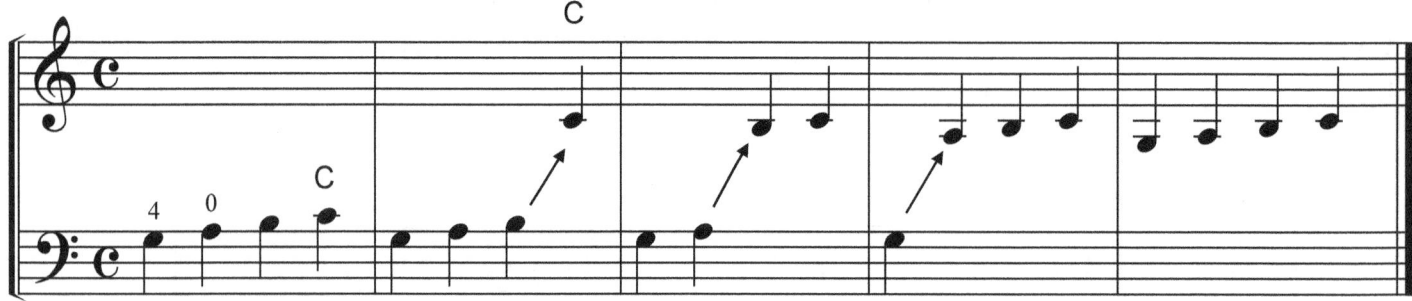

1b. Treble Clef Connections Starting on G (single staff)

When you play this line, see how the same notes
look when they are written on a single staff.

2a. Treble Clef Connections Starting on A (score form)

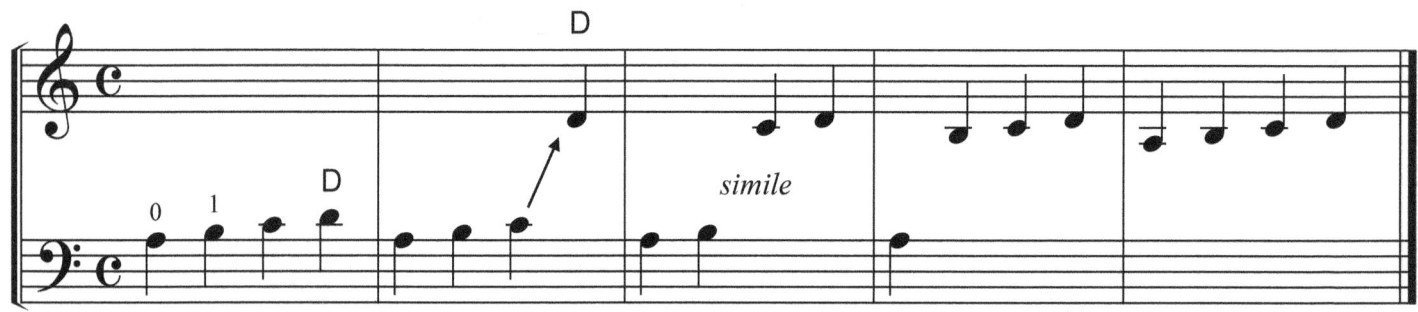

2b. Treble Clef Connections Starting on A (single staff)

3a. Treble Clef Connections Starting on B (score form)

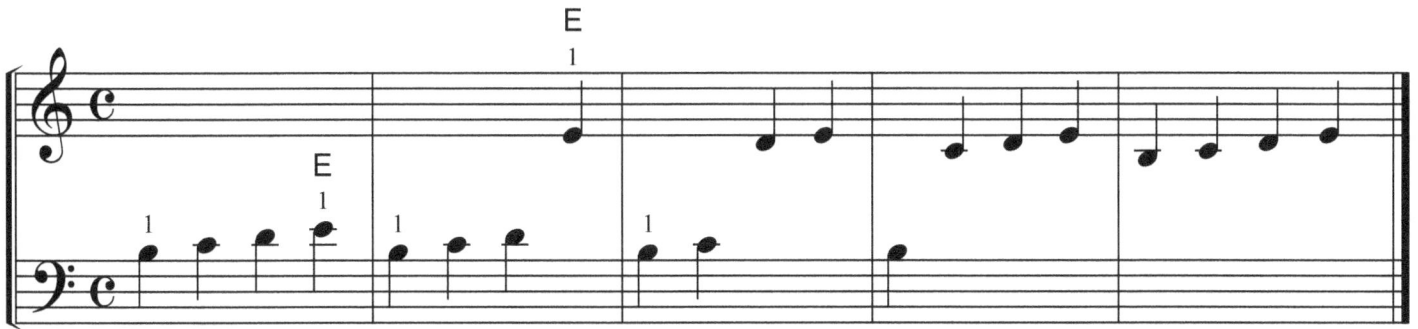

3b. Treble Clef Connections Starting on B (single staff)

4a. Treble Clef Connections Starting on C (score form)

4b. Treble Clef Connections Starting on C (single staff)

The Note "C"
5a. Recognizing "Middle" C in Treble Clef

5b. Recognizing C in Treble Clef (single staff)

6a. Finding C After Playing Lower Notes

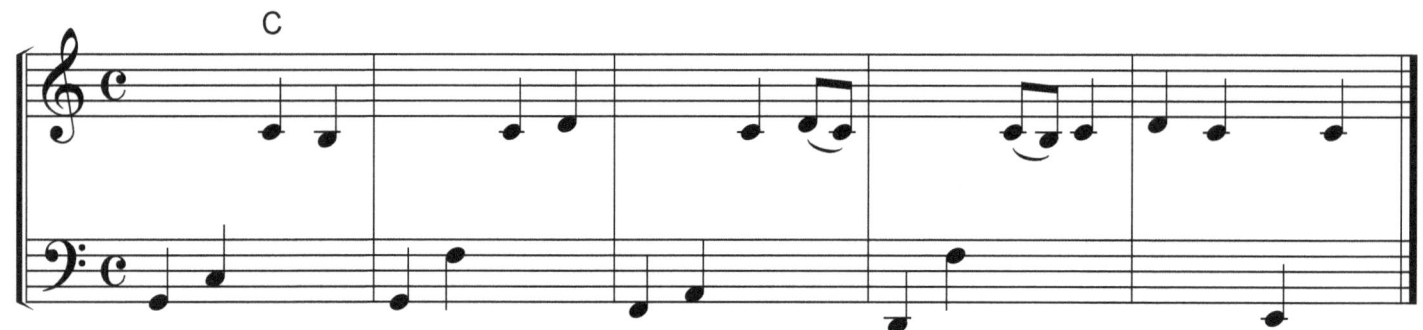

6b. Finding C After Playing Lower Notes (single staff)

7. Etude

©2024 C. Harvey Publications® All Rights Reserved.

8. The Notes Around C

9. German Folk Song

Brahms

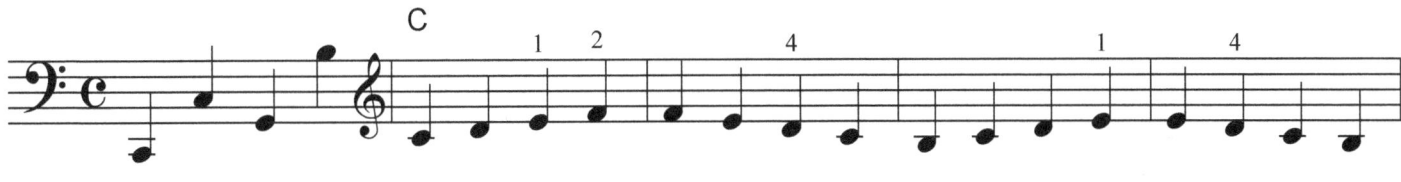

The Note "A"
10a. Learning to Recognize "A"

10b. Learning to Recognize "A" (single staff)

11a. Finding "A" After Playing Lower Notes

11b. Finding "A" After Playing Lower Notes (single staff)

12. Etude

©2024 C. Harvey Publications® All Rights Reserved.

The Notes "B" and D"
15a. Learning to Recognize "B"

15b. Learning to Recognize "B" (single staff)

16a. Learning to Recognize "D"

16b. Learning to Recognize "D" (single staff)

17. Etude: Recognizing "B" and "D" from Different Places

Treble Clef for the Cello

18. Treble Clef Shifting Etude

19. Shifting Exercise

20. Mit Hörnerklang

Breslauer, arr. Harvey

©2024 C. Harvey Publications® All Rights Reserved.

The Note "E"

21a. Learning to Recognize "E"

21b. Learning to Recognize "E" (single staff)

22a. Shifting Around "E": Stay in each position until the next one is indicated.

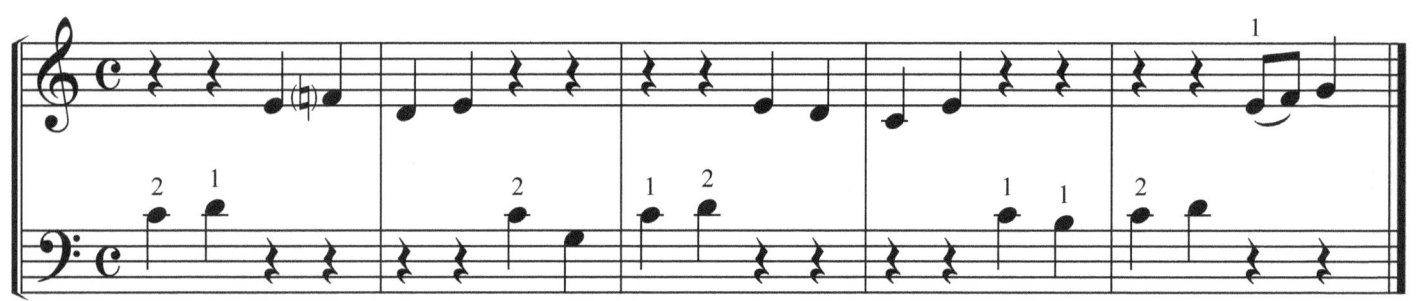

22b. Shifting Around "E" (single staff)

Stay in each position until the next one is indicated.

23. More Shifting with "E"

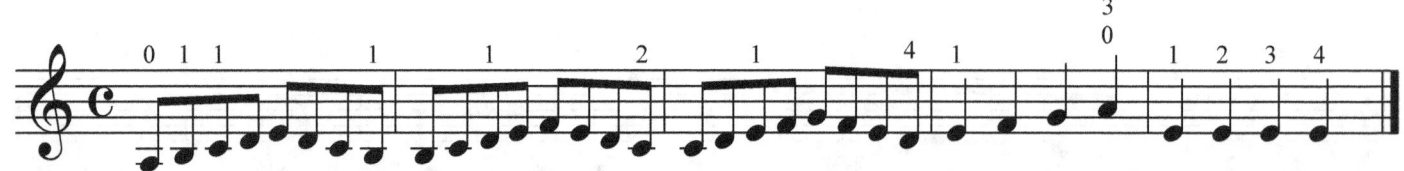

Treble Clef for the Cello

24. German Folk Song
Brahms

Allegretto giocoso

25. Allegro from Sonatina Op. 24, No. 1
Krause

Allegro

©2024 C. Harvey Publications® All Rights Reserved.

The Notes "F" and "G"

26a. Learning to Recognize "F"

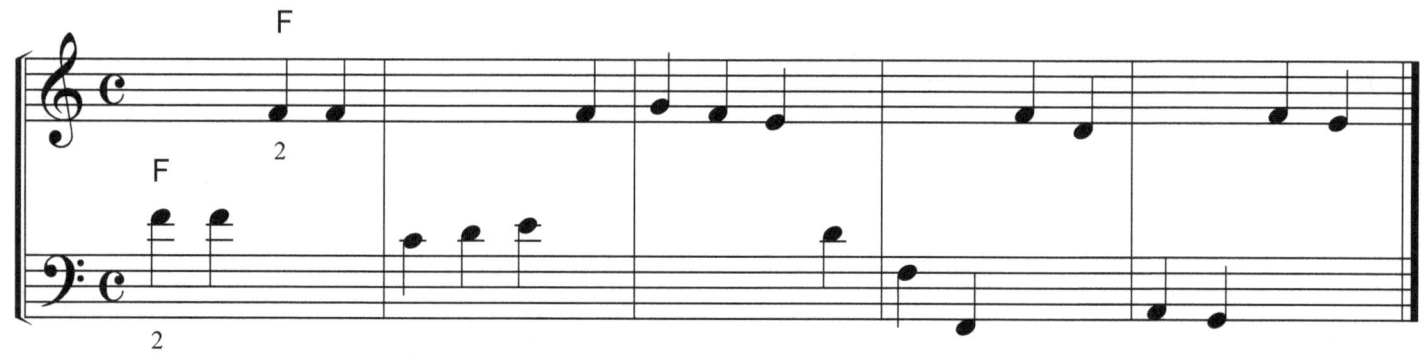

26b. Learning to Recognize "F" (single staff)

27a. Learning to Recognize "G"

27b. Learning to Recognize "G" (single staff)

28. Etude

©2024 C. Harvey Publications® All Rights Reserved.

Treble Clef for the Cello

29. Early Morn
Lanciani

30. La donna è mobile
Verdi

The Note "A"
31a. Learning to Recognize "A"

31b. Learning to Recognize "A" (single staff)

32a. The Notes Around "A"

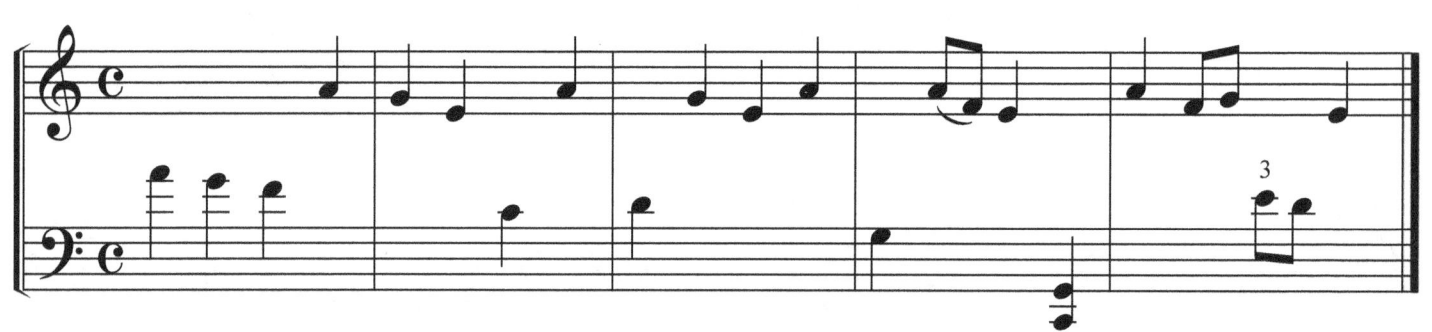

32b. The Notes Around "A" (single staff)

33. Etude in A Major

©2024 C. Harvey Publications® All Rights Reserved.

34. Gavotte
Martini

35. Gavotte Moderne
Tours

Low "G" and Scale Patterns
36a. Learning to Recognize Low "G"

36b. Learning to Recognize Low "G" (single staff)

37. G Scale Patterns

38. F Major Etude

Treble Clef for the Cello

39. Theme from Sonatine in C Major
Loeschhorn
Vivo

40. Polonaise and Menuet
Scholze

41. Focus on Fourth Position Across Strings

42. Fourth Position Double Stop Study

43. Finger Exercise Across Strings

Stay in 4th position for this exercise.

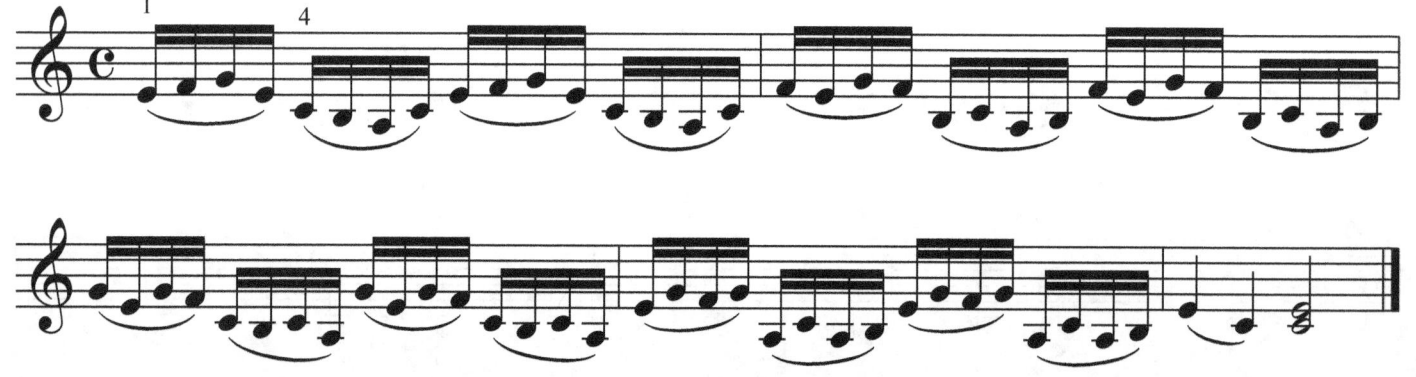

©2024 C. Harvey Publications® All Rights Reserved.

46. Second Position Across Strings

Stay in second position for this entire exercise.

47. Third Position Across Strings

Stay in third position for this entire exercise.

48. Second Position and Third Position

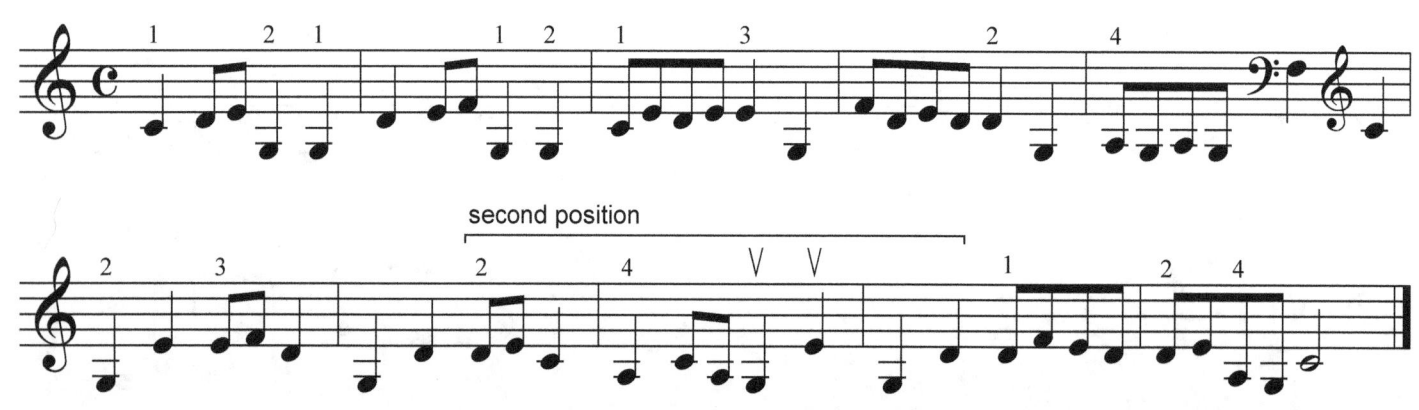

49. Pastorale

Roger-Ducasse

50a. Tenor Clef to Treble Clef Starting on E

Play and read with awareness, seeing how each note looks in treble clef after the tenor clef.

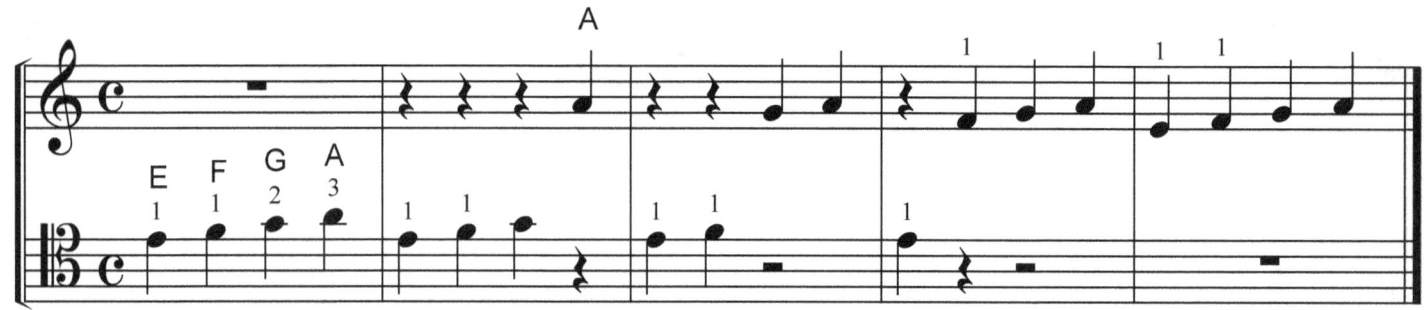

50b. Tenor Clef to Treble Clef Starting on E

Play and read with awareness, seeing how each note looks in treble clef after the tenor clef.

51a. Tenor Clef to Treble Clef Starting on F

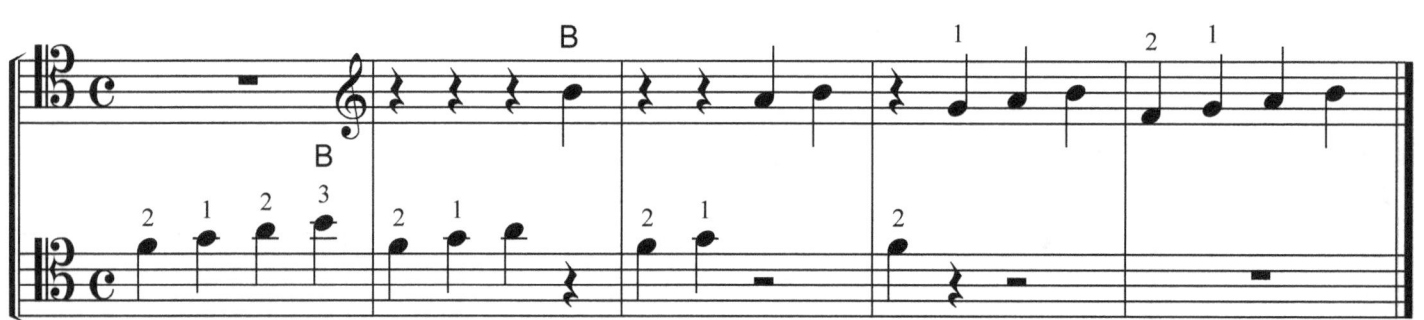

51b. Tenor Clef to Treble Clef Starting on F

Treble Clef for the Cello

52. Sixth Position in Three Clefs

Stay in 6th position for this exercise.

53. Across Strings in Sixth Position

Stay in 6th position for this exercise.

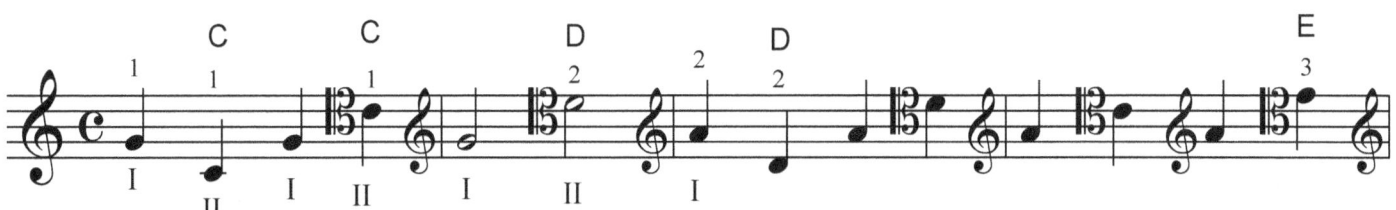

54. March

Harvey

Stay in 6th position for this piece.

©2024 C. Harvey Publications® All Rights Reserved.

55. Learning C in Treble Clef

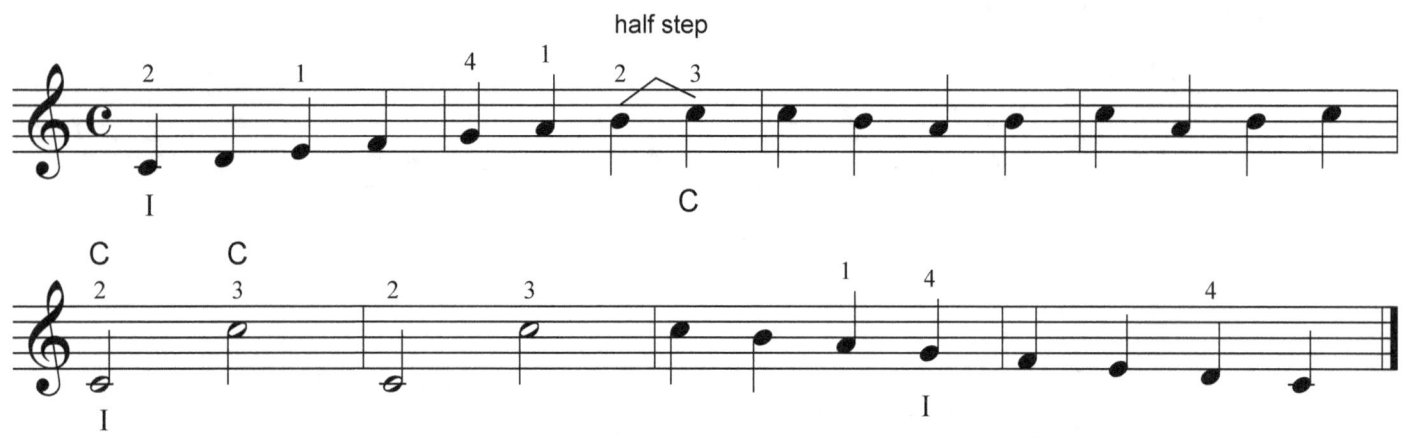

56. Recognizing C in Treble Clef after Tenor Clef

57. Seventh Position Across Strings

58. To a Wild Rose
MacDowell

59. Sumer is Icumen In
Traditional, arr. Harvey

60. Treble Clef in Thumb Position (starting on the Harmonic)

Note: This is a brief overview of treble clef in just one of the positions where we use the thumb.
For a comprehensive study of thumb position, see **Thumb Position School for Cello** (CHP261)

61. Low Second Finger

©2024 C. Harvey Publications® All Rights Reserved.

64. Skipping Notes in Thumb Position

65. Different Intervals in Thumb Position

66. Es, es, es und es, es ist ein herter Schluß

German Folk Song, arr. Harvey

67. Soldier's Joy

Traditional, arr. Harvey

©2024 C. Harvey Publications® All Rights Reserved.

68. Major Scales Up One String

Treble Clef for the Cello

For more material like this, see Scale Studies for the Third Octave, Book One (CHP165) and Book Two (CHP210.)

©2024 C. Harvey Publications® All Rights Reserved.

69. Major Arpeggios Up One String

70. Melodic Minor Scales Up One String

71. Minor Arpeggios Up One String

72. Broken Third Studies

For more material like this, see Broken Thirds (One String) for the Cello, Book One (CHP211) and Book Two (CHP310.)

Treble Clef for the Cello

73. Octave Shifts on the A String

For more material like this, see Octave Shifts for the Cello, Book One (CHP104), Book Two (CHP128), and Book Three (CHP215.)

74. O Mio Babbino Caro

Puccini

75. Learning Harmonics as "Landmarks"

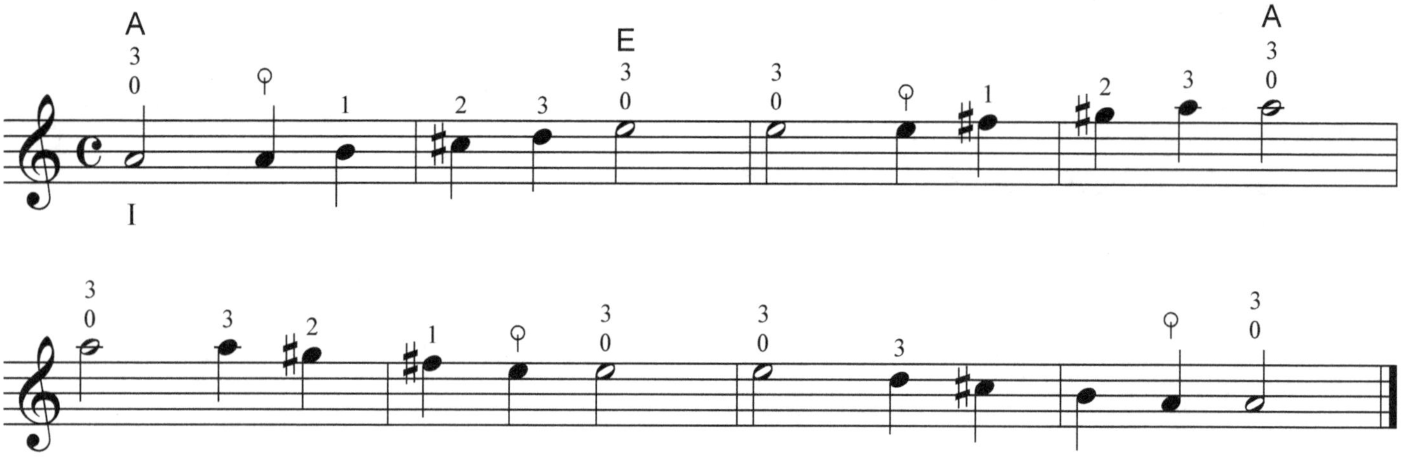

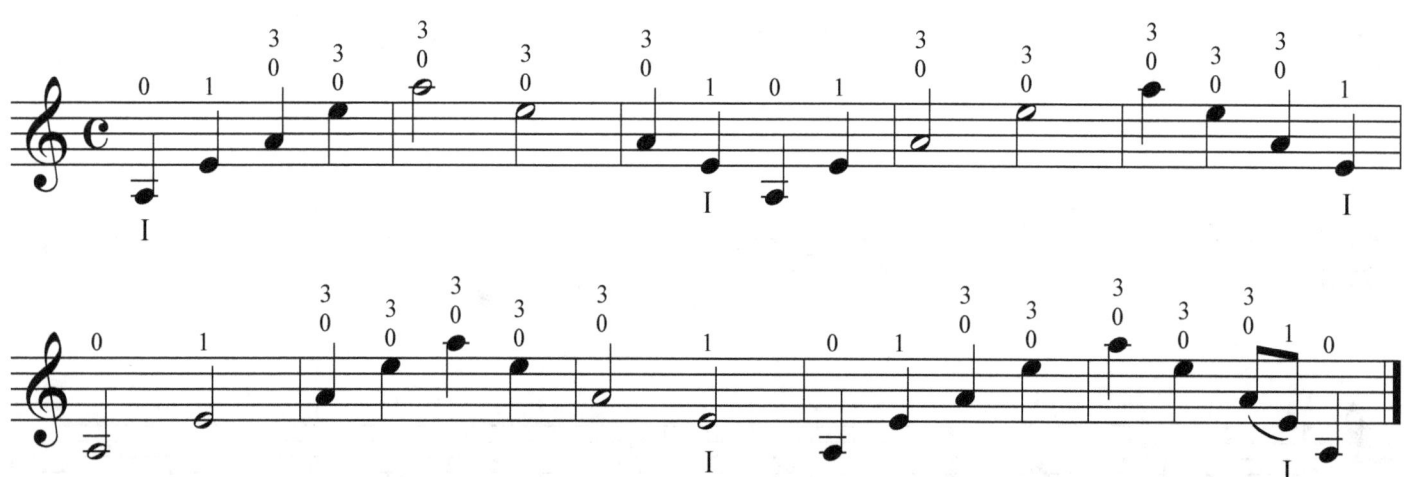

76. "Landmark" Exercises

77. Reading Treble Clef One Octave Lower Than Written

Some composers have parts that are written in treble clef but meant to be played one octave lower. Dvorak and Schumann are examples of composers that have some published music that still includes this "false" treble clef.

Reading treble clef an octave lower is also an extremely useful skill for playing violin music or vocal music that goes too high to be played comfortably on a cello.

In this section, try reading the top line of each exercise one octave (eight notes) lower than it is written, glancing at the lower line only when you are not sure of the note.

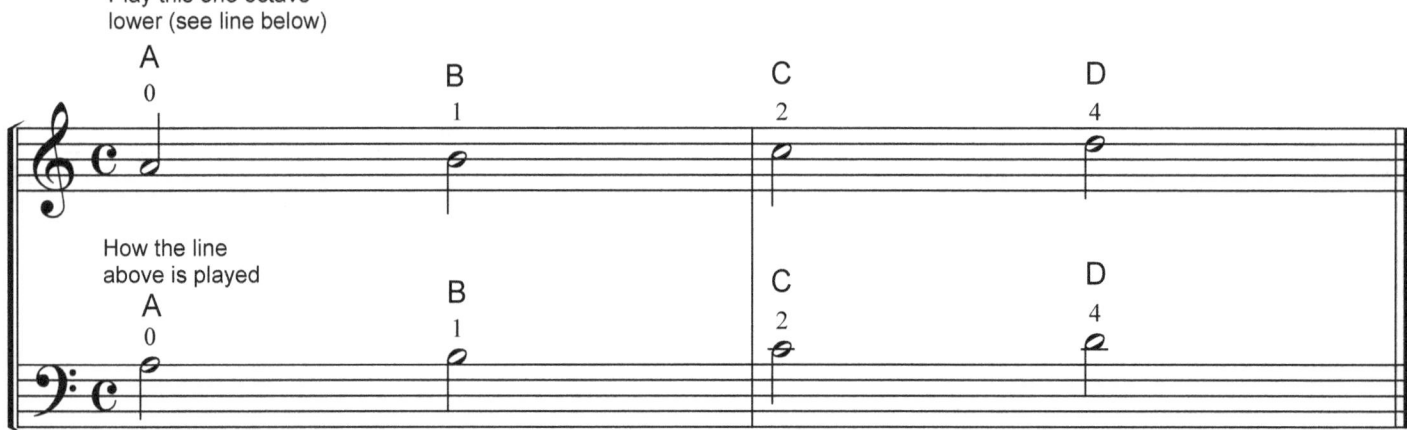

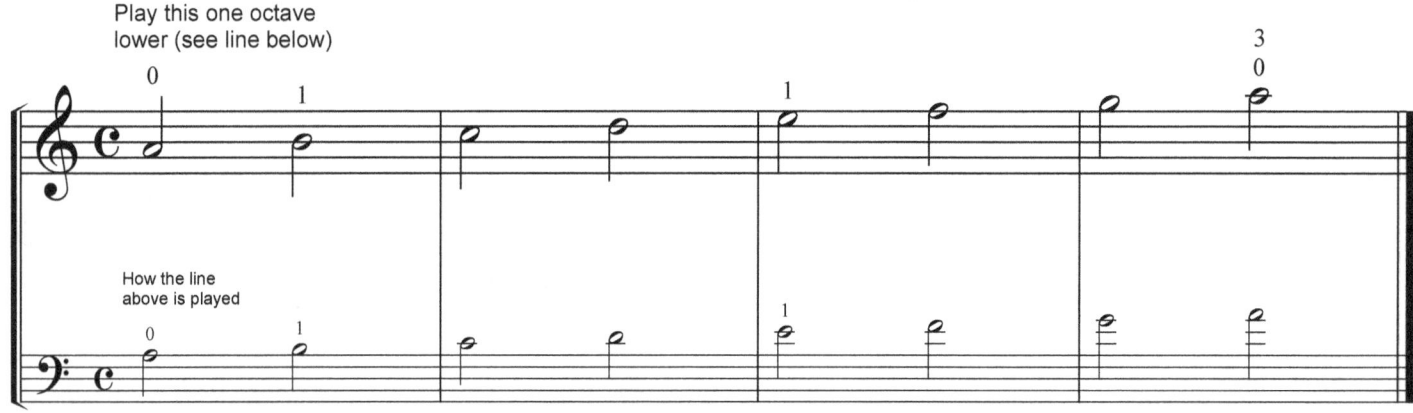

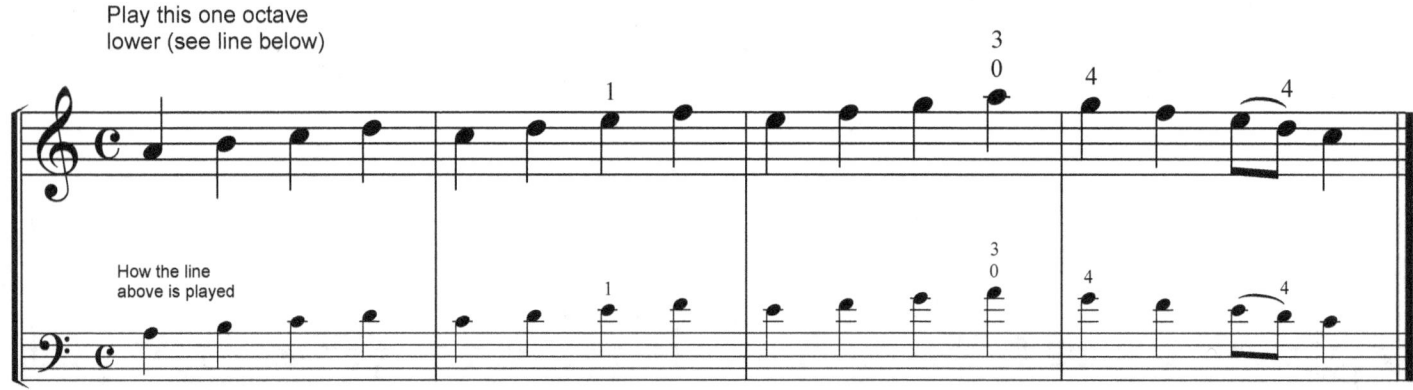

78. Reading Treble Clef One Octave Lower Than Written
Scale Patterns: Reading Notes in Order

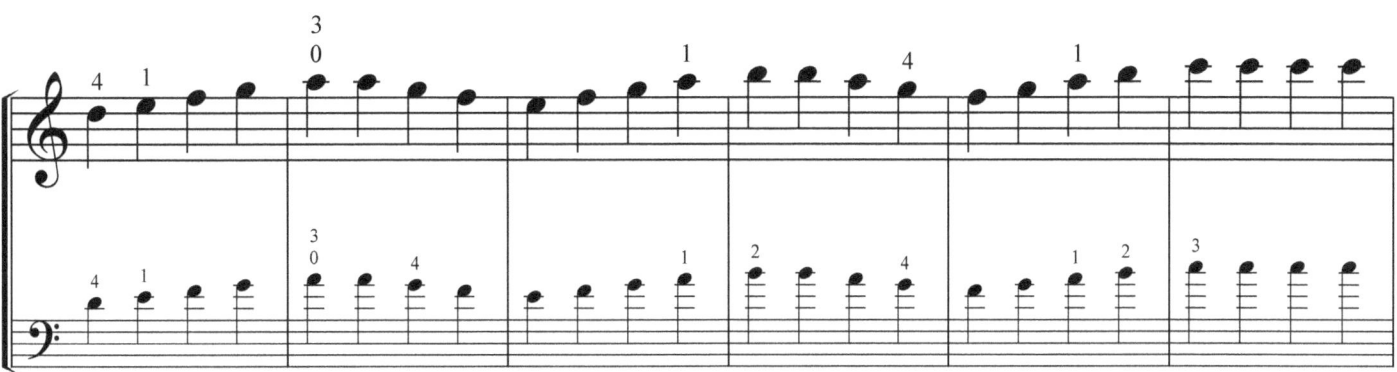

79. Reading Treble Clef One Octave Lower Than Written
Recognizing Thirds

Play this one octave lower (see line below)

How the line above is played

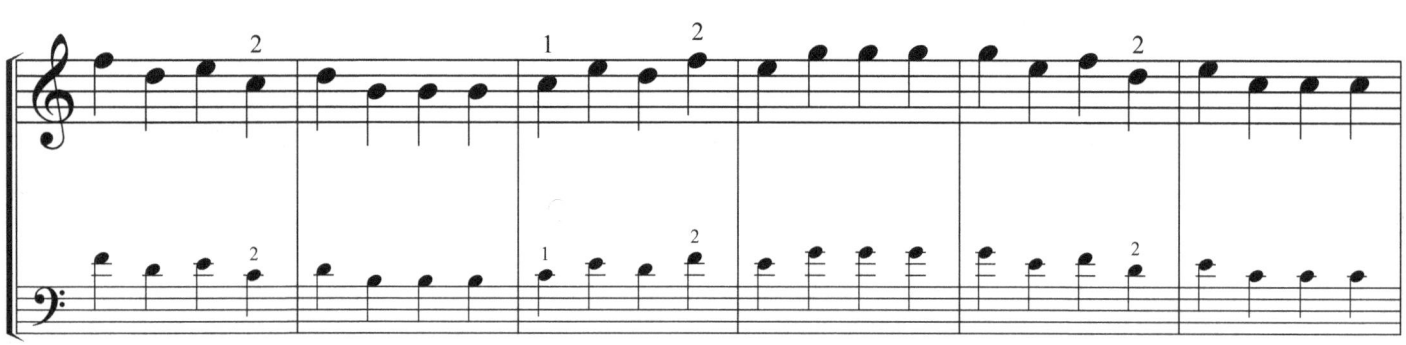
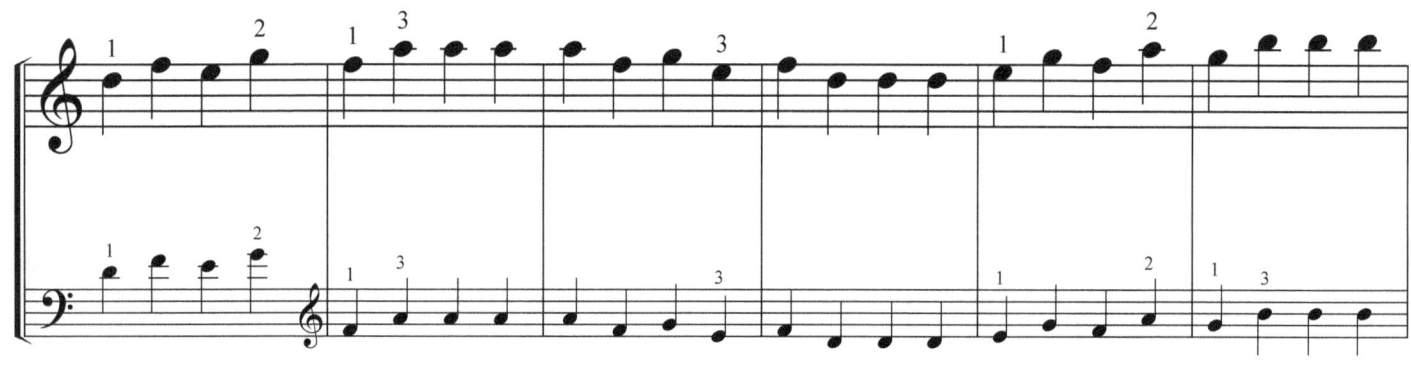
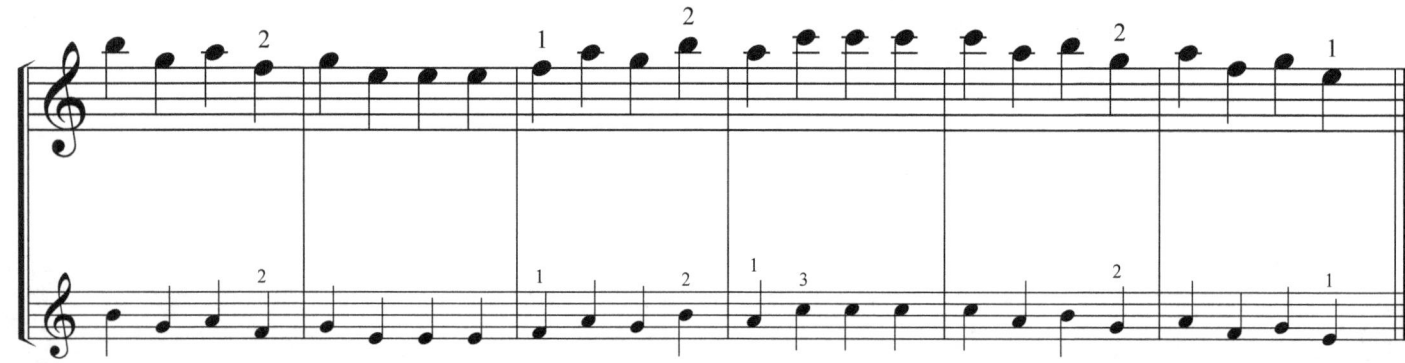

80. Reading Treble Clef One Octave Lower Than Written
Recognizing Fourths

Play this one octave lower (see line below)

How the line above is played

81. Reading Treble Clef One Octave Lower Than Written
Finding Notes After Bass Clef: Think of Note Names as You Play

Play all treble clef notes in this exercise one octave lower than written.

82. More Note Name Awareness

Play all treble clef notes in this exercise one octave lower than written.

©2024 C. Harvey Publications® All Rights Reserved.

Treble Clef for the Cello

83. The "False" Treble Clef in Beethoven's String Quartet Op.18, No.4, Movement 1: After Rehearsal F

Allegro, ma non tanto

©2024 C. Harvey Publications® All Rights Reserved.

84. The "False" Treble Clef in Dvorak's American String Quartet
Movement I, Rehearsal 14, starting at Measure 127

Treble Clef for the Cello

49

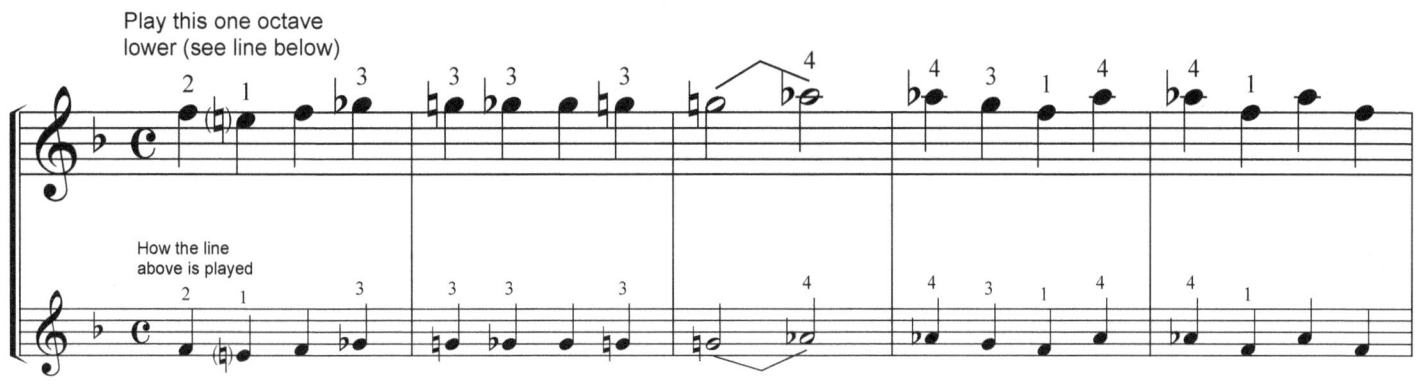

©2024 C. Harvey Publications® All Rights Reserved.

85. The "False" Treble Clef in Dvorak's American String Quartet
Movement I, Rehearsal 15, starting at Measure 140

Treble Clef for the Cello

86. The "False" Treble Clef in Dvorak's American String Quartet
Movement I, Rehearsal 17, starting at Measure 160

Treble Clef for the Cello

Treble Clef for the Cello

Play this one octave lower (see line below)
vibrato on all quarter notes

How the line above is played
vibrato on all quarter notes

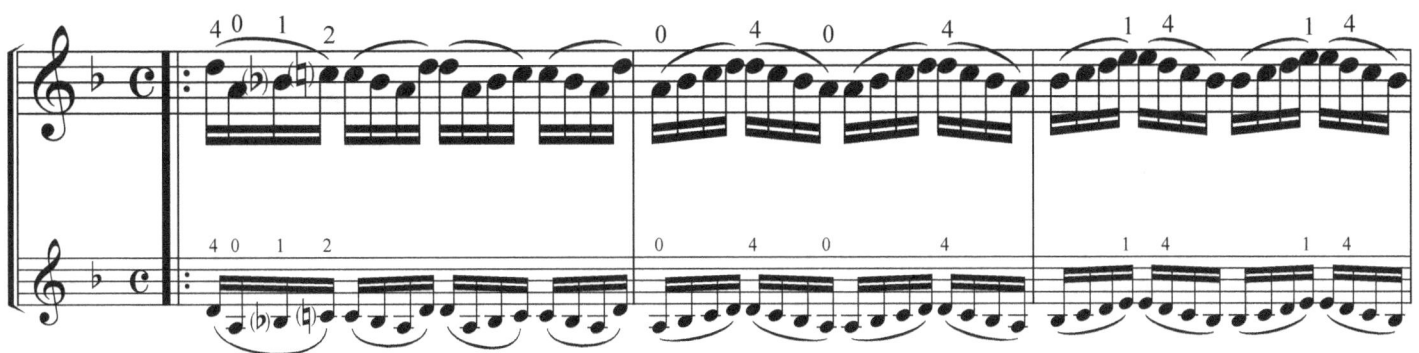

Repeat several times, playing faster each time, until this is played as fast as possible.

Repeat several times, playing faster each time, until this is played as fast as possible.

©2024 C. Harvey Publications® All Rights Reserved.

88. The "False" Treble Clef in Dvorak's American String Quartet
Movement II, Rehearsal 3, starting at Measure 30

Exercises

Treble Clef for the Cello

89. The "False" Treble Clef in Dvorak's American String Quartet
Movement II, Rehearsal 8, starting at Measure 81

Exercise

You Might Also Like
Thumb Position School for Cello: CHP261

Cassia Harvey

Intonation Study

Finger Exercise

©2015 C. Harvey Publications All Rights Reserved.

www.ingramcontent.com/pod-product-compliance
Lightning Source LLC
Chambersburg PA
CBHW082214070526

44585CB00020B/2409